Day of the Cat

Day of the Cat

Kong Hye Jin

THUNDER BAY
P·R·E·S·S
San Diego, California

A precious day, as recorded by one cat's servant.

Her eyes meet mine as I smooth the fur on her face and she gazes at me with light green eyes. As I close my eyes and slowly caress her soft fur, following the soft curve between her head and back, my restless mind calms at the touch. As I sit daydreaming, then turn my head, she is always there, looking at me, her eyes following me attentively.

I often stop what I'm doing—whether laughing, crying, drawing, eating, or even sleeping—to look at her. She and I have become friends. Her name is Bono. She is my beloved cat.

I've recorded the many times when I'm being observed by Bono or when I'm observing her. A full day of such moments appears in this book. While drawing her perfect form, I felt I briefly became my cat. Our relationship even developed to the level where I could understand her "code," and we had a special way of communicating.

Everybody should have his or her own Bono. This book is the result of observing and recording one day in the life of someone precious to me.

Look through Bono's entire day as it is shown in this book, and choose a moment that attracts your attention. Then add colors, little by little. Throughout the day, depending on what you are doing, find a spot in the illustration that captures your attention and color in a detail, one at a time. In that way, you are paying attention to Bono's day.

Finally, thank you, Ms. Bono, for accepting me as your lowly servant.

If you color me in with your heart, I will repay you with my charms.

6:30am

I had a good night's sleep.

I'll have a stretch, and then I think I should wake up my servant to make me breakfast.

Hidden pictures

1 butterfly, 2 ostriches

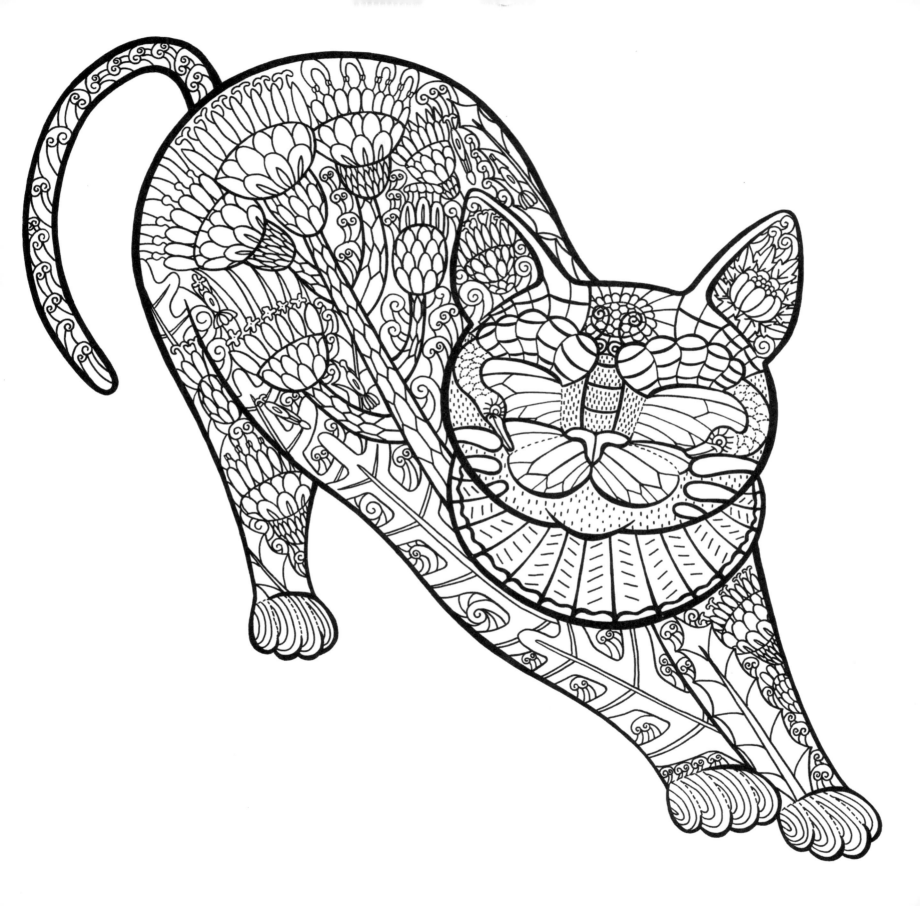

6:50am

Hey servant, wake up!

Why aren't you getting up even though I'm wrapped around your face?

Hidden picture

1 sloth

8:00am

What's this?! How did a grain of steamed rice get stuck here?

Well, I guess I'll eat it.

8:30am

When I sit here like this, nobody can tell me apart from the flowers.

Hidden pictures

2 ostriches, 1 elephant

9:20am

I'm such a nimble hunter.

How could I let that fly get away?

Hidden pictures

1 fish, 2 birds

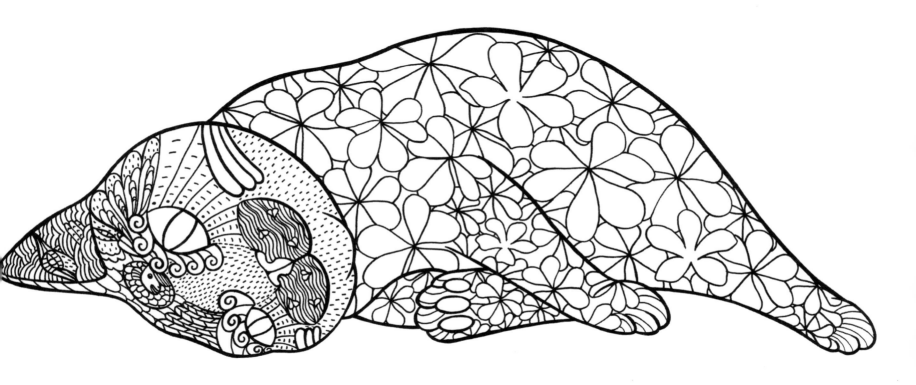

10:30am

A bird is flying outside the window.

Hidden pictures

1 azalea, 1 bird

11:30am

I'm lying down and looking up at the clouds. Ah, that's why people prefer window seats!

Hidden pictures

1 swan, 1 bee

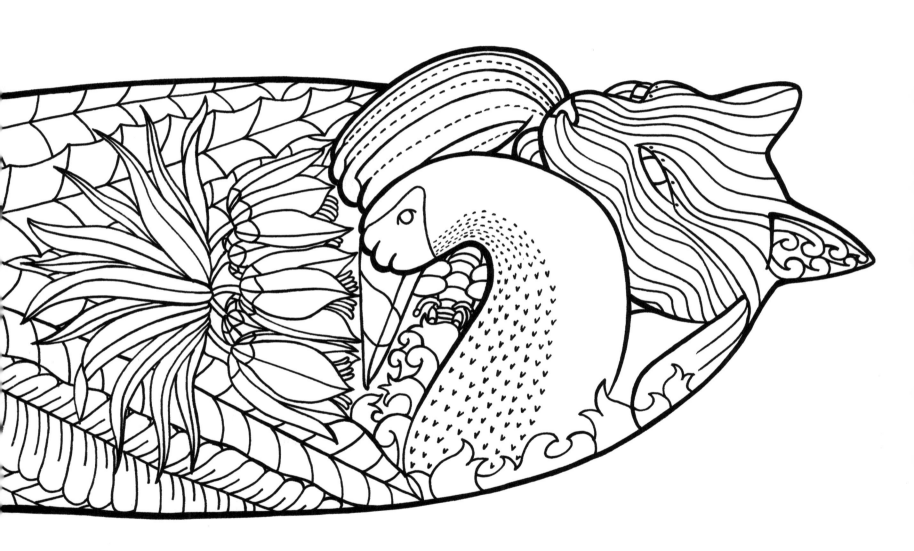

12:10pm

I'm rolling around in the sunlight. It's as wonderful as being in a flower bed.

Hidden picture

1 koala

12:50pm

I shouldn't let my guard down even while taking a nap. I'll arm myself with cuteness!

1:30pm

I need some time to myself. Please don't interrupt me…meow.

2:00pm

Where are you going? I'm all ready!

Hidden pictures

4 bees

2:20pm

I'm not sleeping.

I'm just closing my eyes…

because I'm meditating. Meow.

Hidden pictures

2 owls, 2 fish

2:30pm

My body is perfect. Wherever you look, it's amazing!

Hidden pictures

2 goldfish

3:00pm

A haughty cat posture. Should I try it?

3:30pm

I find myself putting my paws together whenever I imagine something fun.

3:50pm

I'm going to win everyone over with my cuteness!

Hidden pictures

1 zebra, 1 camel, 1 bear

4:00pm

I'm strangely attracted to slippers. What does the servant do with all those slippers?

4:20pm

Each time you bring me something yummy, I'll give you a piece of toilet paper.

Hidden picture

1 peacock

5:00pm

How was your outing, servant? What's my snack going to be?

Hidden pictures

2 ostriches, 2 caterpillars

5:05pm

If I bow my head too long, it will spoil the servant.

So, I'll count to five and stand up.

Hidden picture

1 owl

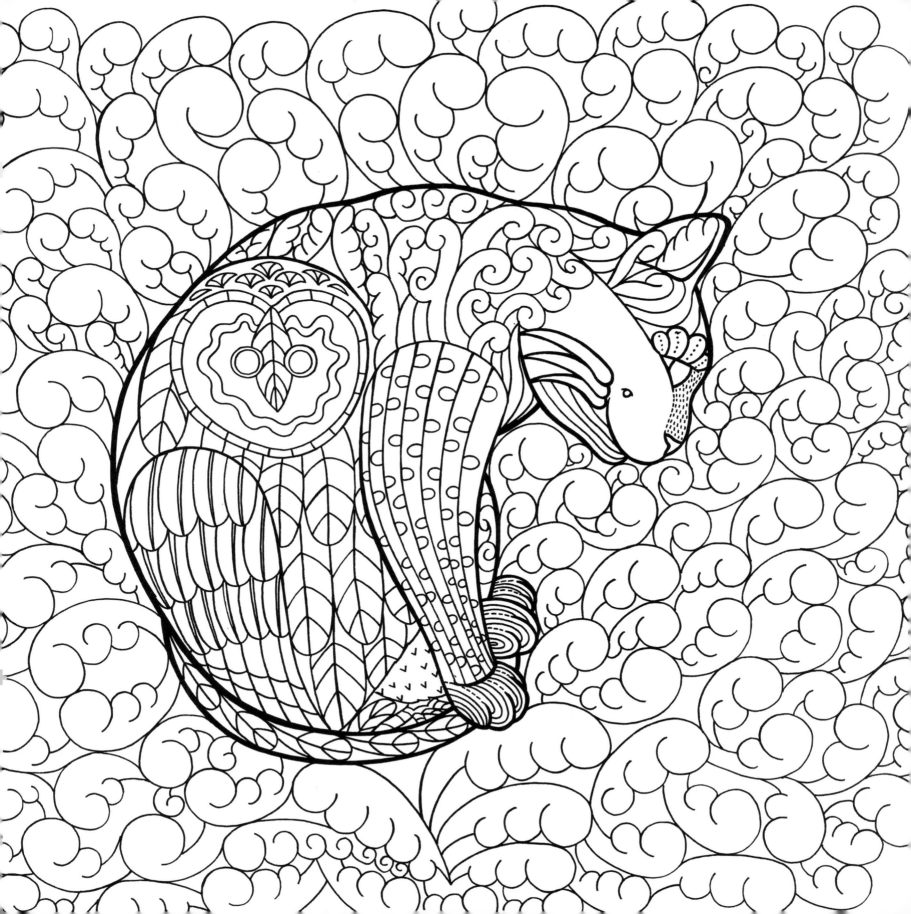

5:30pm

Curl your body up as much as possible, says Bono!

Hidden pictures
1 eye, 1 duck

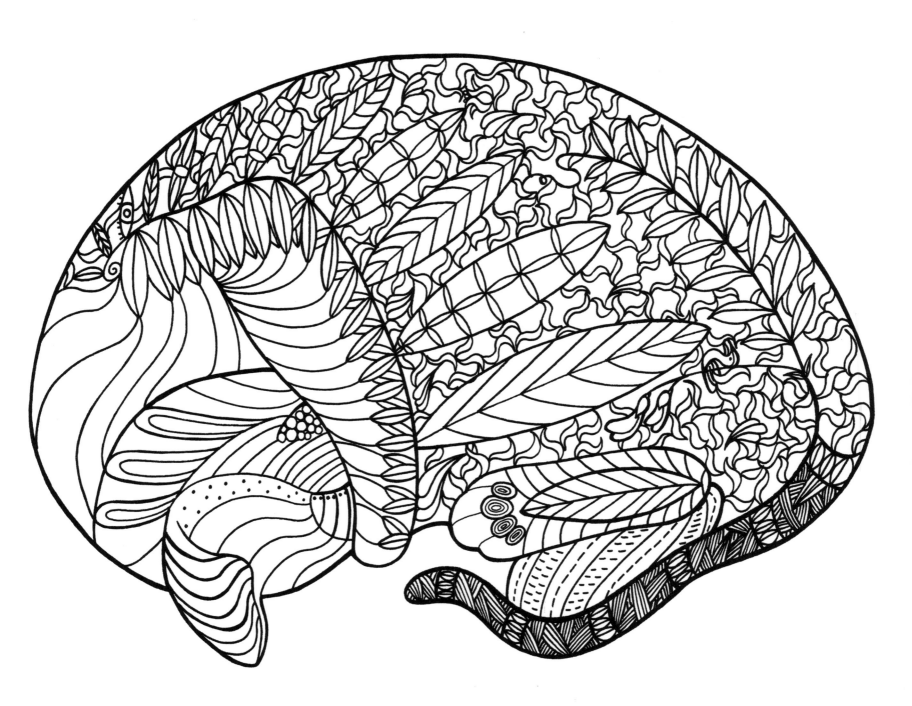

6:00pm

Whenever I see a thread, I automatically turn into a penguin.

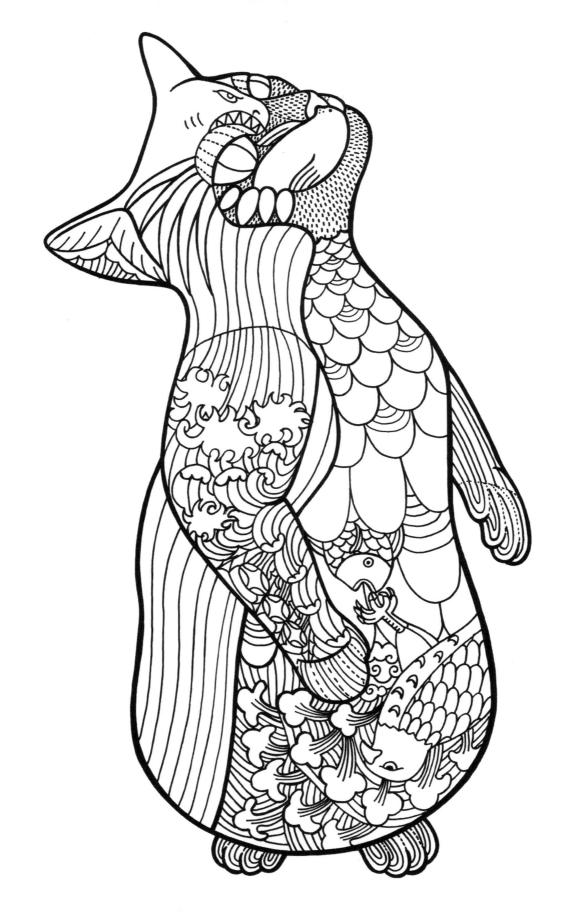

6:30pm

Just wait and see.

As soon as I do this, my servant will run right to me.

Hidden pictures
1 twisted breadstick, 1 ribbon

6:50pm

I'm having a massage in the servant's lap.

Hidden pictures

1 deer, 2 birds

7:00pm

When my picture is being taken, I make myself out to be the cutest cat in the world.

7:20pm

They will think there is a bird in the cat bed.

Hidden pictures

9 birds

7:40pm

I would like to eat with the servant at the table! Meow.

Hidden pictures

1 rabbit, 1 peacock

7:50pm

I'd like to use the "15 Minute Massage" coupon.

Hidden pictures

1 rabbit, 1 bird, 1 llama

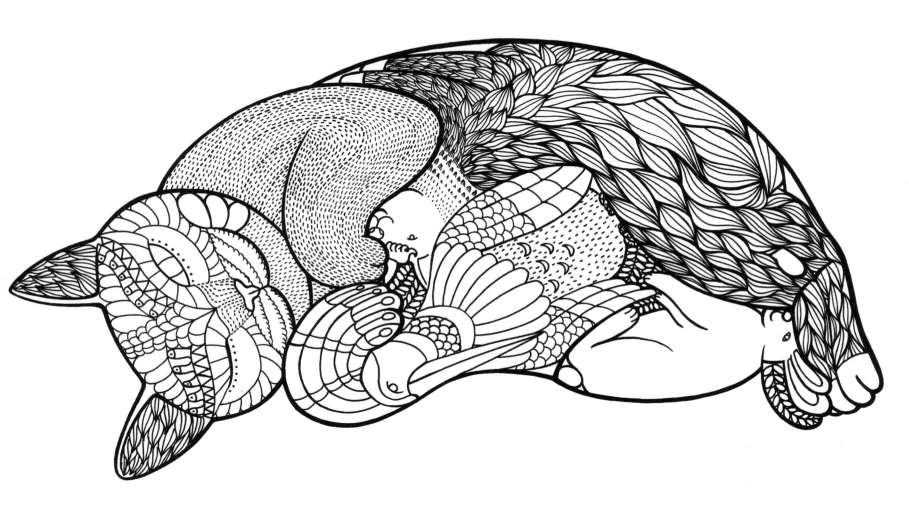

8:00pm

I transformed myself into a glamor puss!

Hidden pictures

1 eagle, 1 seal

8:20pm

When I hug a ball of yarn, I feel like I've been transported to a relaxing world.

Hidden pictures

1 ray, 1 shark, 1 octopus, 3 fish

8:40pm

If you look at me while I'm sleeping, you will find serenity.

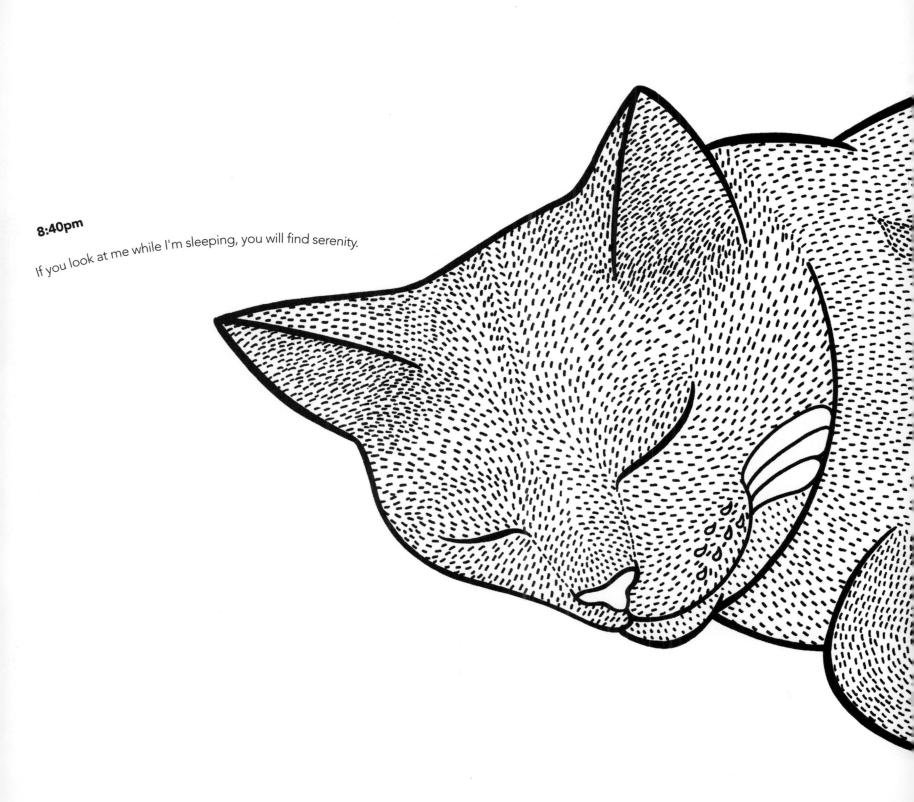

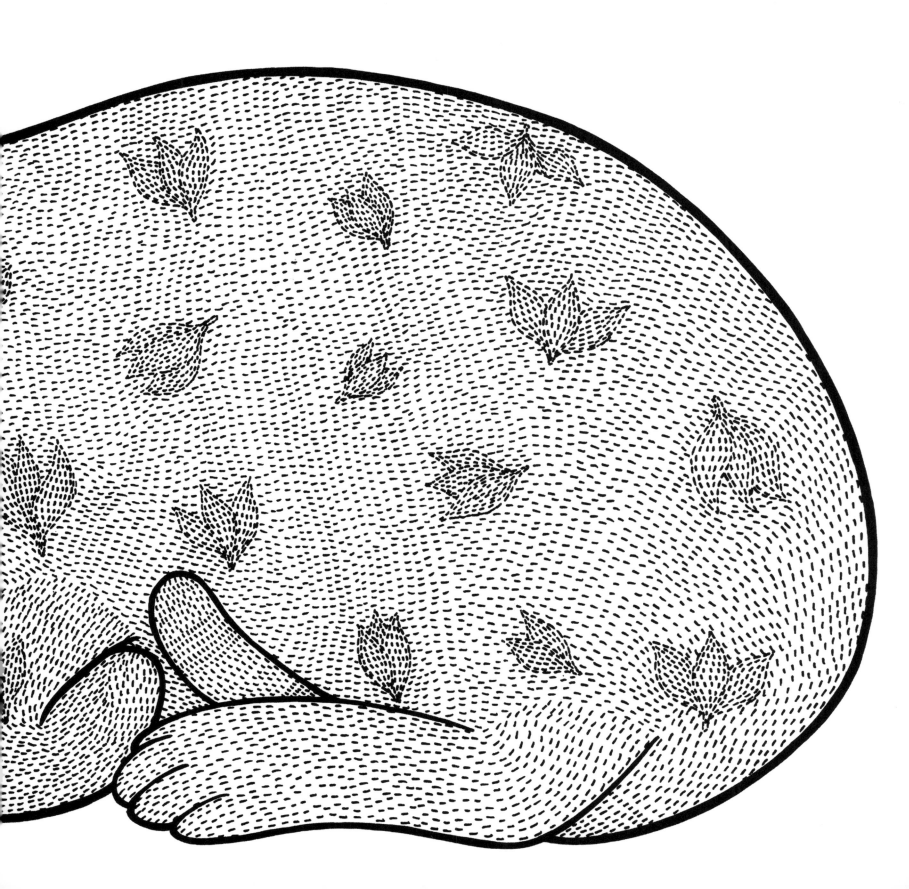

9:00pm

Should I get up? Or lie down?

Oh! I might stay up all night!

9:20pm

When I receive a massage from the servant, I completely relax.

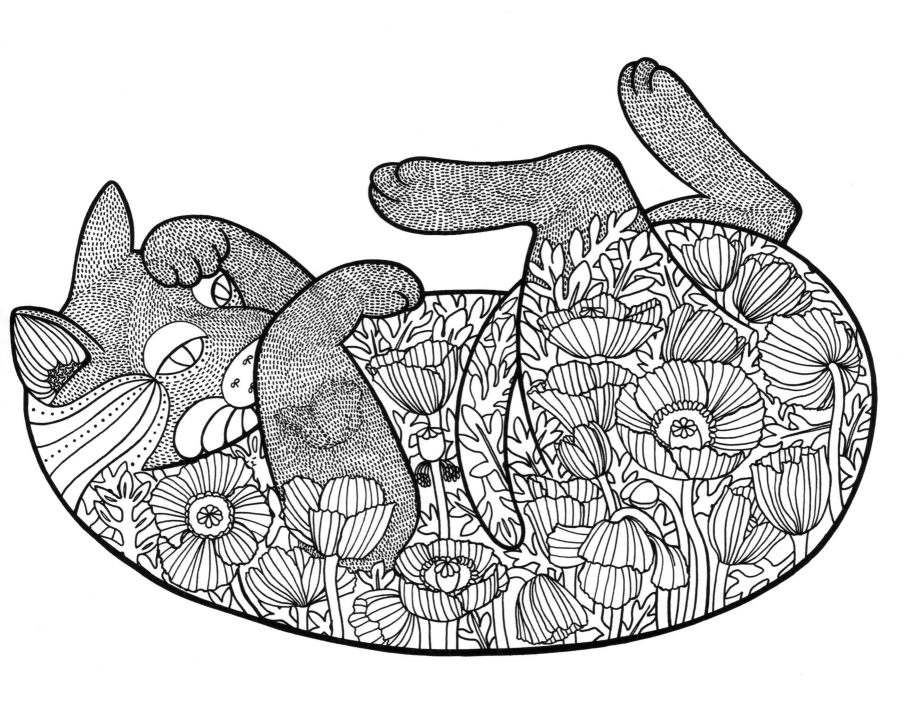

9:40pm Since you gave me such a lovely massage with such devotion, I will repay you with my charms.

Hidden pictures

1 carp, 1 whale

10:00pm

Pet me, pet me, please! Meow.

Hidden pictures
1 bird, 1 ram

10:30pm

When you feel cold and empty, try cuddling me in your arms.

Hidden picture

1 rhinoceros

11:00pm

I transform into an owl at night!

Hidden pictures

2 ducks, 1 owl

11:30pm

Since my servant has gone to bed, I'll sleep too.

I'll run through fields and fly over the ocean in my dreams.

Hidden pictures

1 hawk, 1 octopus, 1 dolphin, 4 fish

12:00am

In my dreams, I keep finding myself in a jungle.

Try writing a letter to someone who is special to you.

Cut along the solid lines.

Fold along the dotted lines, and attach each of the sides using glue to make a pretty envelope for your letter.

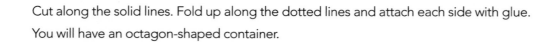

Cut along the solid lines. Fold up along the dotted lines and attach each side with glue.
You will have an octagon-shaped container.

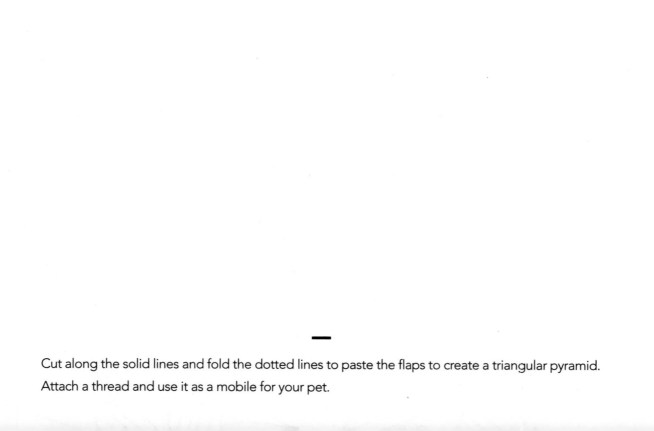

Cut along the solid lines and fold the dotted lines to paste the flaps to create a triangular pyramid.
Attach a thread and use it as a mobile for your pet.

Now draw a moment you had with someone who is special to you.

Thunder Bay Press
An imprint of Printers Row Publishing Group
10350 Barnes Canyon Road, Suite 100, San Diego, CA 92121
www.thunderbaybooks.com

Text and illustrations copyright © Munhakdongne Publishing Corporation 2015
English translation copyright © Octopus Publishing Group 2015

First published in Korea in 2015 by Munhakdongne Publishing Corporation

Printers Row Publishing Group is a division of Readerlink Distribution Services, LLC.
The Thunder Bay Press name and logo are trademarks of Readerlink Distribution
Services, LLC.

All notations of errors or omissions should be addressed to Thunder Bay Press, Editorial
Department, at the above address. All other correspondence (author inquiries, permissions)
concerning the content of this book should be addressed to Octopus Publishing Group Ltd,
Carmelite House, 50 Victoria Embankment, London EC4Y 0DZ

Thunder Bay Press
Publisher: Peter Norton
Publishing Team: Lori Asbury, Ana Parker, Laura Vignale
Editorial Team: JoAnn Padgett, Melinda Allman

Octopus
Senior Production Manager: Katherine Hockley

Day of the Cat
ISBN: 978-1-62686-704-8

20 19 18 17 16   1 2 3 4 5